Preface

I began teaching sugarcraft, an art form that originated in the United Kingdom, nearly ten years ago. The technique involves applying icing to cakes in elaborate ornamental patterns, evoking the look of lace and embroidery, for instance, and creating detailed sugar hearts, flowers, and more. The icing is prepared by mixing powdered sugar with egg whites and then processing this mixture into a clay-like substance to create a sugar paste.

At the school that I opened in 1999, Sugar Decorating Studio ROSEPETAL, many students prepare cakes for birthdays, weddings, and other celebrations. Not long after I opened the school, a student asked if I could help her prepare an ornamental cookie as a gift. A lightbulb went off in my head, and ever since then, I began to create what I call "painted cookies."

Fortunately, I have been blessed with ample opportunities to make such cookies. People have approached me to help them prepare cookie gifts, and I lecture on creating these treats at special events. With so much enthusiasm surrounding the craft, I saw the need to come up with a good, trouble-free way for someone to design painted cookies him- or herself. The solution I eventually came up with is this simple method:

Place a sheet of OPP (polypropylene) or parchment paper over a drawing, trace it with icing, add embellishments, let it dry, and then affix the sugar picture onto a cookie.

This method is based on a technique in sugarcraft known as "runout"; the icing eventually hardens into what's commonly called "royal icing." While this technique is primarily applied for embellishing cakes, in this book I introduce a variation of it that I have fine-tuned for cookie making.

Nervous about your drawing skills? Don't be! You'll find plenty of charming sketches in this book for you to trace. Simply choose and begin. And remember: Making mistakes is half the fun. Once you get used to decorating cookies with the aid of traceable drawings, you can try creating your own original designs. To me, the amusing task of placing finished icing designs onto cookies is as fun and carefree as decorating everyday objects with fancy stickers.

I sincerely hope that this book will open your eyes to new pleasures. Happy icing.

~ Akiko Hoshino

CHAPTER 1

Mastering Basic Icing Techniques

This chapter covers the basics for making simple painted cookies. You'll learn how to do everything, from making and tinting icing to baking the cookies. You'll find tips and techniques for drawing lines, making dots, and even creating marble patterns. Once you can confidently trace various sketches with icing, and have gained mastery of the basic design motifs and of drawing simple shapes, you can create a wide array of painted cookies to your heart's content. This chapter requires practice, and patience, but with an open mind you can have a lot of creative fun!

Icing

There are two types of icing covered in this book: one uses egg whites, the other uses meringue powder. Feel free to choose whichever you prefer.

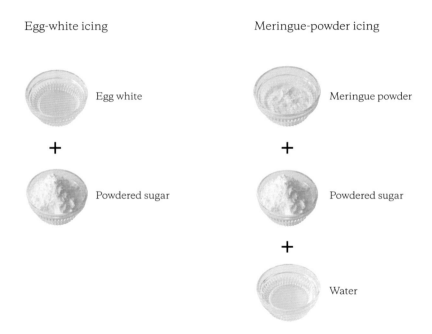

Egg-white icing   Meringue-powder icing

Egg white   Meringue powder

+   +

Powdered sugar   Powdered sugar

                                   +

                                   Water

Tinting

Adding food coloring to your icing produces
a variety of colors for you to have fun with.

Basic Techniques

There are seven basic techniques to learn.

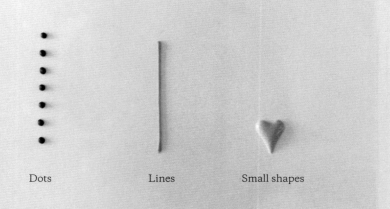

Dots   Lines   Small shapes

Fill Areas

Speckles   Knit stitch   Marble   Basket weave

Tracing

Just place a sheet of OPP or parchment paper over the sketch of your choice and trace it with icing.

Finishing

Once you can fill and overlay, you can produce as many amusing painted cookies as your imagination will allow.

Icing Ingredients and Materials

The ingredients needed for making icing are very basic. In addition to egg white or meringue powder, you only need powdered sugar, water, and food coloring. When preparing (and applying) the icing, work swiftly to prevent the sugar from drying out; keep the necessary utensils handy to ensure a smooth workflow and to save on time.

Ingredients

1. **Powdered sugar:** If possible, use the kind that does not contain cornstarch. Powdered sugar containing oligosaccharide is easy to use.
2. **Egg whites:** Use the egg whites of small-size eggs. Since egg sizes vary slightly, use a scale to measure the weight accurately.
3. **Unsweetened cocoa powder:** Use the sugar-free type for applying color to the icing.
4. **Meringue powder:** Use a brand containing dried egg whites and cornstarch or cream of tartar, a substance that works as a preservative and produces fine-grained bubbles.
5. **Food coloring:** Use to tint the icing. Food coloring comes in two varieties: natural colors derived from plants, and artificial colors derived from oil.

Guide:
1 tablespoon = 0.50 oz
1 teaspoon = 0.17 oz
- For egg white, measure using a scale.
- Icing made with egg white will not last that long. It's best to consume it quickly.
- When baking cookies, the temperature and baking time may vary by the model of oven used, so adjust as necessary.

Tools for Preparing Icing

1. **Bowl:** Use one with a diameter of at least 8 inches and that can accommodate a hand mixer.
2. **Rubber spatula:** Use for mixing the sugar paste and for making the icing smooth.
3. **Measuring spoons:** Use when measuring meringue powder and water.
4. **Scale:** For accuracy, use when measuring powdered sugar and egg whites. A digital model is the most accurate.
5. **Hand mixer:** Apply medium speed. For example, if the marks range from 1 through 5, adjust the setting to 3.

Materials for Applying Icing

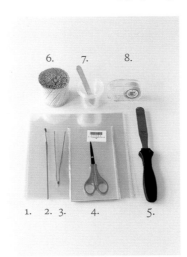

1. **OPP or parchment paper:** Place OPP or parchment paper, or other see-through paper, over a sketch for rendering pictures. Also use this paper to create pastry bags.
2. **Thin paintbrush:** Use a fine-tipped paintbrush lightly moistened with water to smooth out any rough icing edges or to retouch lines.
3. **Tweezers:** Use these to place small pieces of icing and dragées onto the cookies.
4. **Scissors:** Use to snip the tip of a pastry bag, especially if you make your own from parchment paper. A pair with thin, sharp blades is easiest to use.
5. **Palette knife:** Use one with a width of roughly 3/4 inch to mix food coloring into the icing and to fill a pastry bag. A butter knife will also work.
6. **Toothpicks:** Use with filler icing to ensure even coverage and for detailed touch-ups.
7. **Small cup and spoon:** Use when mixing food coloring and when applying tint to a batch of icing.
8. **Adhesive tape:** Use to seal a pastry bag.

Egg-White Icing

Egg-white icing is easy to prepare. Since eggs vary in size, use a scale to accurately check that the egg weighs 1 ounce, even if it is labeled as small. Store the prepared icing in a refrigerator, and make sure to use it within 4 to 5 days.

Ingredients

7 oz powdered sugar
1 oz egg white (1 small-size egg)

1.
Put the powdered sugar into a small bowl and add the egg white.

2.
Using a rubber spatula, mix until the powdered sugar is fully absorbed into the egg white.

3.
Beat with a hand mixer on medium speed until glossy, about 5 minutes.

4.
Scoop up the icing, checking to see if it sticks to the blade of the hand mixer.

5.
Scrape down the sides of the bowl with a spatula and mix to combine.

6.
Once the mixture is smooth, with a consistency rich enough for it to stick to the spatula when scooped up, the process is done.*

A finished batch of icing can dry up quickly when exposed to air, so keep it covered with plastic wrap.

Meringue-Powder Icing

Icing made without raw egg whites will last around 2 weeks if stored in a refrigerator. It has a light texture. If you are reluctant to use raw egg whites, choose this type of icing.

Ingredients

7 oz powdered sugar
1 tbsp meringue powder
2 tbsp plus 1 tsp water

1.
Put all the ingredients into a medium bowl and mix with a rubber spatula until the powdered sugar fully blends into the water.

2.
Beat with a hand mixer on medium speed until the entire mixture becomes lustrous, about 5 minutes, then scrape down the sides of the bowl with a rubber spatula.

3.
Once the mixture turns glossy and smooth, with a consistency rich enough for it to stick to the spatula when scooped up, the process is done.

■ Varying the Icing Consistency

When using icing to paint your cookies, you'll need at least three different consistencies to produce different results: a thick consistency for drawing outlines and other major lines; a medium consistency for drawing minor lines and creating some shapes; and a thin, or soft, consistency for filling up the areas within the lines. Keep in mind that the recipe in this book yields a thick icing. Prepare medium and thin consistencies by adding small amounts of water until the desired consistency is reached.*

Thick consistency

Medium consistency

Thin consistency

This is the standard consistency for the basic preparation. Use this for drawing firm lines, such as borders, and when applying the icing to a piece of cookie.

This degree of thickness prevents the filler icing from spreading too much. Use this when squeezing onto surfaces without borderlines, and when applying the icing to a piece of cookie.

More a liquid than a paste, this thickness allows the icing to drip gently and smoothly. Use it as filler.

Storing Icing
Place the prepared icing in an airtight container and cover with plastic wrap. Place the lid over the plastic wrap and store the container in the refrigerator or freezer. Egg-white icing will last 4 to 5 days in the refrigerator and 1 month in the freezer. Meringue-powder icing will last a little longer: up to 2 weeks in the refrigerator and up to 2 months in the freezer. When using a batch of icing stored in a freezer, first let it thaw in the refrigerator, then stir it again thoroughly before using.

*Since icing with an altered consistency breaks apart over time (especially, one with a thin consistency), make sure to use it the day you prepare it.

Tinting the Icing

A batch of basic icing is white. To add color, mix a small quantity of food coloring*
into the water prior to mixing the icing. However, for the color brown, directly add cocoa
into the finished icing and mix.

Using Artificial Food Coloring   *Using Cocoa*

1.
Put 3 tbsp each of food coloring and water into a small cup. Stir until the desired color is reached and the color is evenly blended.

2.
Put 1 oz icing into another small cup, and add a small quantity of the mixture made in step 1.

3.
Mix well with a spoon.

1.
Place 1 oz icing into a small cup and add 1 tsp cocoa.

2.
Mix well with a spoon. If the mixture is thick, add a very small amount of water to thin it out.

*Artificial food coloring typically comes in standard blue, red, and yellow, which means you can easily make green, orange, and purple by combining equal amounts of two colors. Natural food coloring, however, may have subtle variations in shade, so when you try to create a third color from two, you may not get the same result every time. For this reason, you may want to find purple and green tints ahead of time.

The colors used in this book are all light in tone. Using the palette below as your guide, feel free to combine the colors of your choice. The sample for a light tone of purple is not shown here, since the color is difficult to produce, and you will only get a grayish quality when the quantity of the mixed colors is small. To cut down on time, use one nonporous container (washable plastic, metal, or glass bowls and cups) for each color you want to use. If you use just one bowl —or a paper cup—your work may take longer.

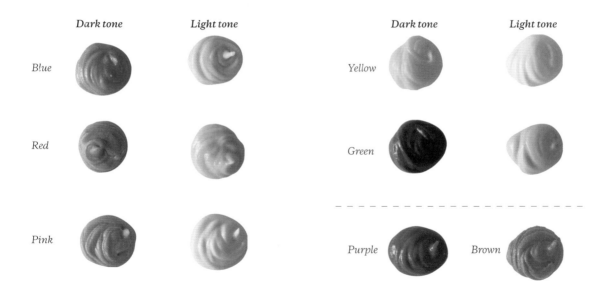

Dark tone *Light tone* *Dark tone* *Light tone*

Blue

Red

Pink

Yellow

Green

Purple   Brown

Applying the Icing

A pastry bag is used to squeeze out icing. You can make your own bag by following these easy steps.

Making the Pastry Bag

1.
Fold a sheet of OPP or parchment paper diagonally to form a triangle, then cut along the fold.

2.
Position the center of the longest side as the top, and roll the sheet to form a cone.

3.
Tape the side of the cone closed with cellophane tape.

 If you'll be using a pastry tip, cut off the point of the cone 3/4 inch from its tip and insert the pastry tip from the wide end before filling with icing.

Filling the Pastry Bag

1.
After mixing the icing well, scoop 1 tbsp icing into the bag with a palette knife.

2.
With the side of the cone with the adhesive tape facing away from you, hold the top of bag and fold the sides toward you, ensuring that all the air escapes and none enters back into it.

3.
Roll from the top down and seal with adhesive tape.

Squeezing Out the Icing

Cut the tip of the pastry bag carefully with a pair of sharp scissors. Depending on where you cut, the volume of icing that you squeeze out will vary—the more you cut off, the more icing will come out with each squeeze.

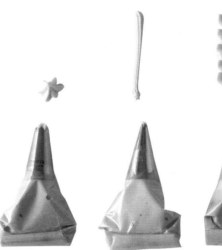

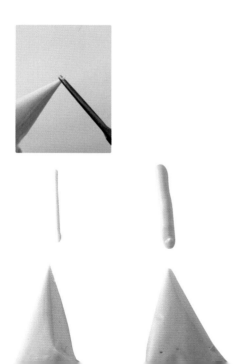

Pastry tips (left to right):
Floral tip: 0.7 in by 1.4 in by 0.2 in; used for creating cupcake-like cookies, as shown on page 81.
8-star tip: 0.7 in by 1.4 in by 0.18 in
Leaf tip: 0.7 in by 1.4 in by 0.2 in; used for creating flower basket-shaped cookies and wreath-shaped cookies, as shown on page 50

Should you need to set the pastry bag full of icing aside for any length of time, cover it with a wet towel, or plastic wrap, to prevent it from hardening.

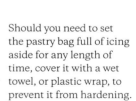

Basic Icing Techniques

To paint with icing, you should first master eight basic techniques.
Once you do so, drawing any type of picture will be a breeze.

Dots

1.
Place a sheet of OPP or parchment paper over the sketch. Using a pastry bag filled with thick-consistency icing, squeeze out tiny polka dots onto the paper, following the lines of the drawing beneath it.

2.
After a few seconds, lightly tap the icing with a thin paintbrush* moistened with water to smooth any jagged edges or fine points on the dots—ideally you're trying to achieve tidy, round dots.

*The paintbrush should be slightly damp. If it is too wet, the icing will become too thin. After wetting the brush, wipe off any excess water before using.

Lines

1.
Place a sheet of OPP or parchment paper over the sketch. Using a pastry bag filled with thick-consistency icing, squeeze out onto the paper, following the lines of the drawing beneath. Keep a steady, smooth flow of icing by gradually raising the tip of the pastry bag.

2.
When you reach the end of the line, slowly lower the tip.

Small Shapes

1.
Place a sheet of OPP or parchment paper over the sketch. Using a pastry bag filled with medium-consistency icing, squeeze out onto the paper, staying inside the lines of the drawing. Fill the space by moving the tip of the pastry bag from right to left.

2.
Tidy up the edges with a thin paintbrush dampened with water.

Fill Areas

1.
Place a sheet of OPP or parchment paper over the sketch. Using a pastry bag filled with thick-consistency icing, squeeze out bold lines onto the paper, following the outline of the drawing beneath. Let dry for 10 minutes. Fill another pastry bag with thin-consistency icing and squeeze out from right to left to fill the area within the outline.

2.
Evenly spread the icing across the area using a toothpick.

Marble

Speckles

1.
Follow directions for "Fill Areas." Before the filler icing dries, fill another pastry bag with thin-consistency icing in a contrasting color and squeeze out thin horizontal lines across the filled area.

2.
Bisect the lines by dragging a toothpick across them vertically from top to bottom. This makes a scale pattern.

3.
Drag the toothpick vertically across the lines again, but in the opposite direction— from the bottom to top—creating a marble pattern.

1.
Follow directions for "Fill Areas." Before the filler icing dries, fill another pastry bag with thin-consistency icing in a contrasting color and squeeze out various size dots across the filled area. The speckles should seep into and be level with the filler icing, not be raised.

Knit Stitches

1.
Place a sheet of OPP or parchment paper over the sketch. Using a pastry bag filled with thick-consistency icing, squeeze out a tiny diagonal line.

2.
Squeeze out another tiny diagonal line across the previous line, forming an X. Repeat steps 1 and 2, slightly overlapping the second X. Repeat until a column of slightly overlapping X's, or stitches, appears, then repeat to make a second column, and so on.

Basket Weave

1.
Place a sheet of OPP or parchment paper over the sketch. Using a pastry bag filled with thick-consistency icing, squeeze out evenly spaced short horizontal lines, forming a narrow column of lines. Then squeeze out one long vertical line, connecting the right edges of all the horizontal lines.

2.
Create a second column of evenly spaced short horizontal lines to the right of the first set of lines—except position each of the lines so that they extend from the empty spaces between the lines of the first column. Then squeeze out another long vertical line against the right edges of the short lines in the second column. Repeat step 2, creating a basket weave pattern, until the drawing area is sufficiently covered.

Finishing

Once you have the hang of the basic design techniques, you are ready to add embellishments and then affix the hardened icing to the cookie. Refer to the photographs and sketches in this book for guidance and inspiration, or feel free to create your own original sketches and embellishments. Adding ornamental detail to your painted cookies, such as the darling adornments on the bear costumes on pages 38 and 39, may be done either directly onto the dry icing of the main picture or by squeezing them out onto OPP or parchment paper first, then adhering them to the main image once dry. Discover what you're comfortable with, and which method works better for your picture, by trying both.

Making a Dress

1.
Place a sheet of OPP or parchment paper over the sketch, fill a pastry bag with thick icing, and squeeze out to trace the outline.

2.
After the outline dries a little, about 10 minutes, fill a pastry bag with thin icing and squeeze out to fill.

3.
Evenly spread the icing across the surface using a toothpick. Let dry for 5 minutes.*

4.
Squeeze out thick icing in a contrasting color to create dainty details.

5.
Once the icing picture is finished, let it dry completely, about 1 day.**

6.
Carefully remove the paper. If the paper sticks, let the icing dry longer, until the paper removes easily.

7.
Squeeze out a few dots of thick icing onto the center of the cookie, then place the dress onto the cookie. Let dry.

Making a Flower

1.
Place a sheet of OPP or parchment paper over the sketch, fill a pastry bag with thick icing, and squeeze out a dot to serve as the center of the flower.

2.
Flatten any rough edges with a thin paintbrush.

3.
Squeeze out several ovals in a contrasting color around the circle, forming petals.

4.
Flatten any rough edges with a thin paintbrush.

5.
Let dry about 10 to 15 minutes.

6.
Draw a face onto the center of the flower. Let dry completely and remove the paper.

7.
Squeeze out a dot of thick icing onto the center of the cookie and place the flower onto it. Let dry.

 *Dry the icing designs on a flat surface. Placing your work on a desk pad is convenient, since you can move it easily. When drying many designs, keep a number of these pads on hand.

 **Handling your designs before they are completely dry could cause dents or cracks. For this reason, dry them on a flat area and under low humidity.

Making Home-Made Cookies

Were you worried that you'd be wasting a bunch of egg yolks making egg-white icing? Well, you shouldn't be, because this cookie recipe calls for egg yolks—not a single egg is wasted making these goodies. Since painted cookies are best achieved with the flattest surface possible, be mindful of rolling out the cookie dough evenly; also take care to prevent slippage—painted cookies don't earn their names if their icing falls off!

Ingredients
7 tbsp unsalted butter at
  room temperature
$^2/_3$ cup powdered sugar
1 egg yolk
$^1/_2$ tsp vanilla
$1^3/_4$ cup flour

1.
Preheat the oven to 350°F. Put the butter into a medium bowl and mix with an electric hand mixer until creamy.

2.
Add the sugar and continue to mix until well blended.

3.
Add the egg yolk and vanilla, and mix until combined.

4.
Sprinkle in the flour and mix until combined. (If making chocolate dough, also add cocoa if making cinnamon dough, add cinnamon.*)

To make chocolate dough, add 2 tbsp cocoa. To make cinnamon dough, add 1 tsp cinnamon, and use $^1/_3$ cup brown sugar in place of powdered sugar.

5.
Mix quickly until the dough is crumbly but holds together when squeezed.

6.
Once the mixture is moist, form into a ball and cover with plastic wrap. Put in the refrigerator for about 15 minutes.**

7.
Place a sheet of parchment paper onto the table, and put a third of the dough onto it. Place another sheet of parchment paper over the dough and roll out with a rolling pin to a thickness of 1/4 inch. To get a uniform thickness the foolproof way, use spacers.

8.
Cut out cookies using a cookie cutter.

9.
Remove the cookie dough surrounding the cutouts.

10.
Place the parchment paper with the cookie cutouts on it onto a cookie sheet and bake until lightly golden around the edges, 10 to 15 minutes.

11.
Remove from the oven and, while still hot and soft, lightly press down on them with the bottom of a baking pan or other flat object to flatten slightly, creating an even, flat surface for the icing topper.

12.
Repeat until all the dough is used, or until you bake the desired quantity of cookies.

If the cockie dough is refrigerated for too long, the dough may become too hard to roll out. In this case, leave the dough standing at room temperature for a little while before rolling out.

Using Store-Bought Cookies

Some boxed cookies are certainly adorable. It's fun to decorate them with just a bit of icing, especially those shaped like animals. You will be amazed at how you can embellish ordinary store-bought cookies, turning them into cute little works of art. Making your own painted cookies from scratch is a wonderful task—but trying out different store-bought varieties, especially in unusual shapes, can be just as pleasing.

Choose store-bought cookies that are hard and flat. Since some prepackaged kinds tend to crumble easily, experiment with several brands until you find one that will carry your icing picture without breaking apart.

cake   honey

Center: bear-shaped cookie featuring icing details of a chef
Right: rectangular cookies with mini pictures and handwriting

Trimmings
Decorating cookies with dragées, gold leaf, dried fruits, and other edible embellishments can create gorgeous effects. When using dragées, add them to the icing with tweezers. When decorating with powders, simply sprinkle them onto the icing. In the case of dried fruits, slice them into small pieces before applying.

CHAPTER 2

Easy Painted Cookies

Basic painting techniques can be incorporated into decorating cookies with fabulous results. By simply combining the methods for drawing dots, lines, and fill, which you learned in Chapter 1, you can create charming shapes, numbers, and letters. With practice, your cookie masterpieces will become easier to create and more fun to make.

Small Shapes

Babies in Bonnets

The hats of these happy siblings are created with dots, and the faces are drawn last. Notice the similarities to the flower on page 27. If you can make that flower, you can make these smiling babies.

It's a . . . Baby!

Serve these adorable cookies at a baby shower, or box them up and give them to the expecting couple as a gift. You'll be exercising the small shape technique described on page 27. You already know how to make that flower!

Dial Up

You can have fun playing games with these number cookies. For instance, ask your child, "Which cookie is number 5?"

ABCD FG
HIJK MN
PQRSTU
WXYZ
& LOVE !?

Say What?
Create cryptic messages by combining letters.
It'll take some practice to create strokes in
varying thicknesses, but you'll get there.

Autumn Leaves

This prancing fawn is mostly filler icing, while the leaves are more defined with clearly drawn outlines.

Ribbons and Lace

Frilly fun can be had playing around with line, knit, and dot
motifs (see pages 22 and 25 for a refresher), transforming
basic circles and squares into ornamental treasures.

Sugar Bears
Start with a simple, solid-color bear, and then let your imagination soar!

Have fun designing outfits for any occasion—and don't forget to accessorize.

Find Inspiration in Your Child's Artwork

Children's sketchbooks are filled with wonderful images perfectly suited to icing. There's something so amusing about the drawings that kids create. Adults simply can't compete with the breezy innocence inherent in children's artwork.

The painted cookies shown are similar to the doodles I found in my son's sketchbook. Following the steps laid out in this book, I simply placed an OPP sheet over one of his drawings, traced the lines in icing, and then adhered the dry icing to the cookie with a small dot of fresh icing. I am very pleased with the result. Aren't the cookies simply adorable? When I placed them on the table, my son became very excited and exclaimed, "Look, these are like my pictures! That's Hee-kun, that's Shun-kun, that's Yamato-kun, and oh, that's Miyo-chan!" As you can imagine, I was very happy seeing my child's face light up with so much joy. The moment was priceless.

Cookies like these can certainly spark lively exchanges between you and your child. Your bond can grow stronger, so why not give it a try?

Sketches and drawing tips for pages 32 and 33.

The face in the center is drawn with a blend of light shades of red and yellow.

The antennae can break easily if drawn too finely, so be careful.

The beak's color is made from a touch of red and dark yellow.

For the wings, squeeze out icing beginning from the outside toward the inside.

This simple, cute shape can be used over and over. Have fun experimenting with different colors.

First squeeze out icing for the face and body, then overlay the ears, mouth, hands, and legs.

First squeeze out icing for the bottle and its tip, then overlay the lines.

Although the pattern shows only one sock, make a pair and place them next to each other. They will look adorable.

For the rattle, squeeze out colors separately, then overlay the lines.

For a smooth finish, use the speckles technique. But if you want the dots to be raised and pronounced, use the dot technique.

When squeezing out the dots for the sleeve and leg cuffs, make sure they are touching, otherwise they may break apart when you try to transfer the dry icing to your cookie.

First squeeze out icing for the face, body, and hat, then overlay the dots.

First squeeze out icing for the main bib area, then overlay the dots and bow.

First squeeze out the fill areas, then overlay the lines.

First complete the base portion, then overlay the dots and lines.

First squeeze out the main body, then overlay the lines.

Making Sketches from Cookie Cutouts
Place a cookie cutter on a sheet of OPP or parchment paper. Trace the inside of the cookie cutter with a pencil. Remove the cookie cutter and draw a bold outline with a marker slightly inside the outline you just sketched. Then draw any other details that strike your fancy to complete the sketch. Now you're ready to squeeze out the icing!

41

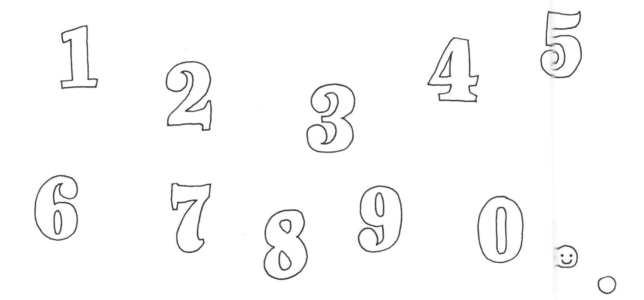

These sketches are designed for beginners, so the width of
the numbers is slightly wider than the ones seen in the photo.
Once you become adept in applying icing, feel free to adjust
the thickness of the lines.

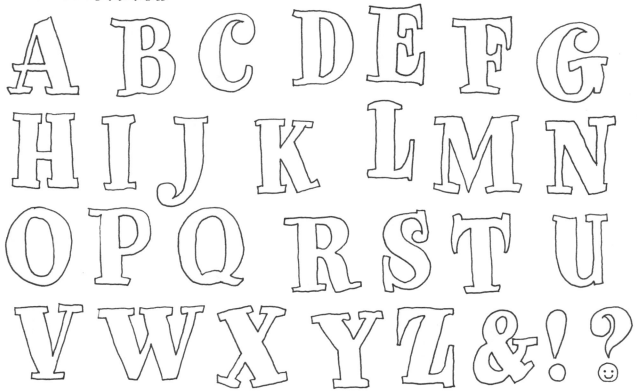

These letters are also sketched in a wider style than those shown in the photo, making them easier for beginners to master. When filling them with thin icing, make sure air bubbles do not enter the pastry bag and pass into the icing.

Did you notice how the icing covers pretty much the entire surface of each cookie in the photo? Read the sidebar "Making Sketches from Cookie Cutouts," on page 41, to learn how to achieve this beautiful look.

Sketches and drawing tips for page 37.
First squeeze out icing for the entire surface using the technique
for fill areas on page 23. Then overlay the lines and dots after the
fill areas have dried completely.

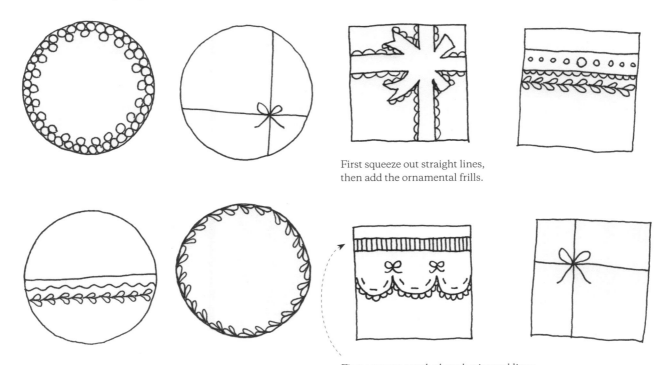

First squeeze out straight lines,
then add the ornamental frills.

First squeeze out the long horizontal lines,
then add the short vertical ones.

Sketches and drawing tips for pages 38 and 39.

Begin these outfits by tracing the main outlines in thick-consistency icing and then filling the area with thin icing in the same color. Once dry, you can overlay all of the darling details: crowns, caps, and bonnets; belts and pockets; collars and cuffs; and shoes.

Since the fill areas are wide, be wary of air bubbles. If they start to rise, burst them with a toothpick.

47

Edible Gifts

A single decorated cookie presented as a gift can brighten anyone's day. When giving cookies as presents, put them in a jar or plastic container to prevent the icing from crumbling. A clear container, strategically placed on a table during teatime, is ideal for displaying your masterpieces. Your friends can gaze at them in awe before nibbling. While elaborate wrapping is conventional for an attractive presentation, the icing itself will do just fine in conveying your good wishes.

CHAPTER 3

Advanced Painted Cookies

Ready to try more elaborate designs? This chapter takes the basic fill, line, and dot techniques you learned in Chapter 1 to another level by incorporating speckle, basket weave, and stitch patterns. Let everything from flowers to freight trains be your inspiration. Have fun!

Baskets and Wreaths
Make the small flowers one by one very carefully, referring to "Making A Flower" on page 27.
Use two different pastry tips to squeeze out the basket weave pattern and the leaves.

Flower Power

The layered flower petals are made with the aid of a paintbrush. Using multiple colors adds a gorgeous effect.

Sketches and drawing tips for pages 50 and 51.

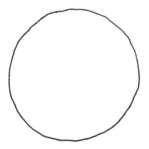

Make the wreath and trimmings separately. To make the wreath, squeeze icing along the circular outline with a leaf-decorating tip. Let it dry, then affix the ornamental flowers.

When drawing the basket handle with dots, squeeze them out so that they are touching. Once the body of the basket is filled with icing, follow the Basket Weave directions on page 25. Squeeze out the leaves with a leaf-decorating tip, and overlay the flowers at the end.

Render the petals from the outside in, then squeeze out the center last.

Squeeze out dots without leaving gaps to prevent them from breaking apart when removing them.

Since the dark purple of this flower and the berries tends to fade, overlay it after drying thoroughly.

To render the small flowers, squeeze them out with an 8-star decorating tip. Position the pastry bag vertically over the surface, and squeeze directly onto the paper. Tidy up rough edges with a thin paintbrush.

First squeeze out the background color—one large circle. Make the flowers and hearts separately.

For the petals, use icing with a medium consistency. Squeeze out following the outlines, using slightly more than the usual amount, then spread the icing toward the center with a thin brush. This will give the borders a raised effect. Once the outside petals are dry, squeeze out the inner petals in the same way.

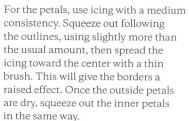

At the Beach
So many colorful beach sandals. Which one to choose?

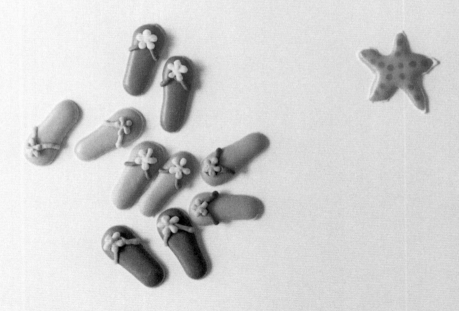

Speckles, marble, and line patterns add a vibrant look to these bikini babes.

Squeeze out lines after
creating the sandal surfaces,
then affix flowers last.

Use these basic bikini
shapes as the fill area.

 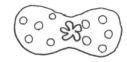 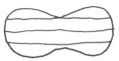

Before the filler icing dries, squeeze out stripes in a complementary color.

Create marble patterns by making swirls with a toothpick.

Add lace, bows, and flowers last.

 Render the leopard design by applying the same technique used to make speckles (see page 24).

Trucks, Trains, Ships, and More
By air or by sea, it's time to take a trip!

Get a move on with these speedy mobiles, plus a high-soaring balloon.
The kids will surely be thrilled.

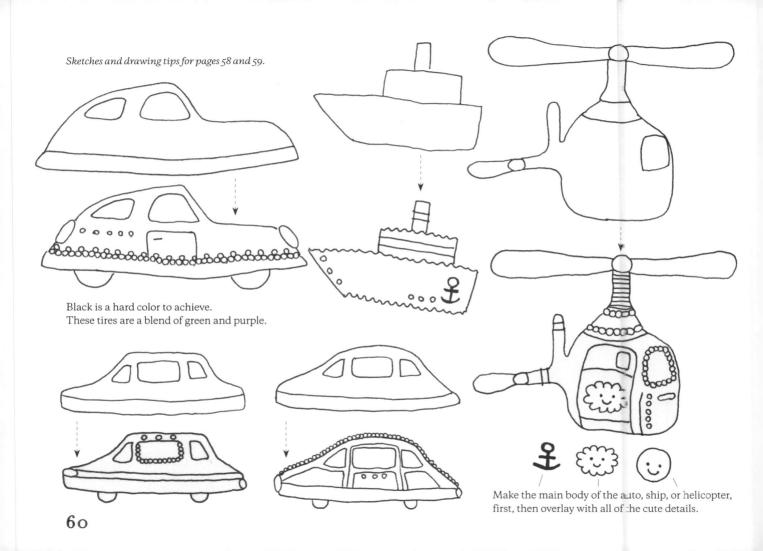

Sketches and drawing tips for pages 58 and 59.

Black is a hard color to achieve.
These tires are a blend of green and purple.

Make the main body of the auto, ship, or helicopter, first, then overlay with all of the cute details.

60

For these shapes,
trace the outlines
first, add in
thin icing, then
overlay dots and
lines last.

Wintertime

Get comfy with wintry motifs. Using darker colors enhances the cool-weather ambience.

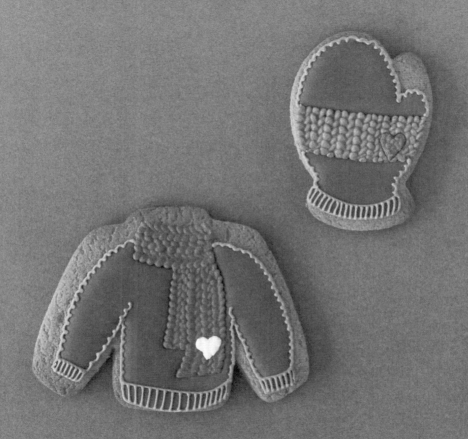

The knit pattern looks realistic, doesn't it?
It evokes a warm and cozy feeling.

63

Sketches and drawing tips for pages 62 and 63.

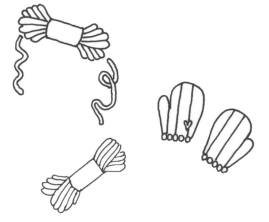

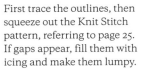

First trace the outlines, then squeeze out the Knit Stitch pattern, referring to page 25. If gaps appear, fill them with icing and make them lumpy.

For the buttons, pierce holes with a toothpick before the icing dries.

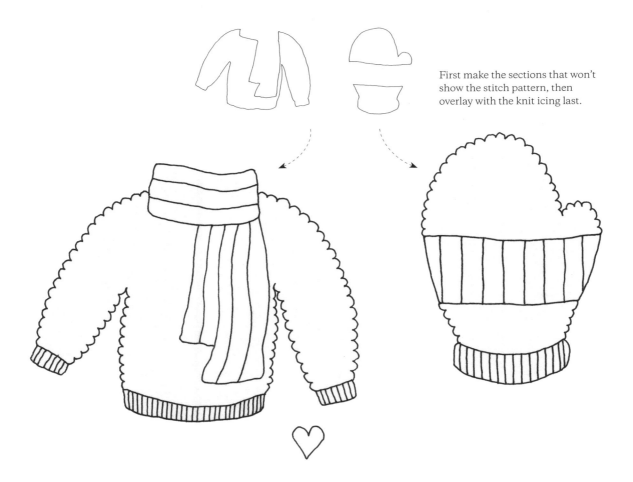

First make the sections that won't
show the stitch pattern, then
overlay with the knit icing last.

65

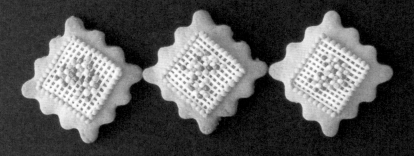

The intricate latticework is the masterstroke of this design's charm.
After the cross-stitch-like patterns dry, arrange the flowers.

Heart-shaped cookies exude happiness and love.
Create the right balance by positioning the flowers at the bottom of the pattern.

Sketches and drawing tips for pages 66 and 67.

Create the lattice pattern with white
icing, squeezing out horizontal lines
first, then overlaying with vertical ones.

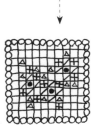

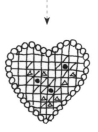

- •   Red
- ∕   Light red
- +   Green
- △   Light green

Overlay the dots using the
patterns as your guide.
It's fine if they move slightly
out of position.

CHAPTER 4

Special Occasion Cookies

Are you ready to show off your new talent? Everyone loves cookies, and they make such thoughtful gifts. Whether you prepare them for a major holiday, or offer them as a birthday gift to that special someone, your cookies will surely put smiles on everyone's faces. This chapter presents ideas for common special occasions, but the sky's the limit when it comes to reasons for gift giving. Let's discover a marvelous array of heartwarming cookies!

BIRTHDAY

What could be inside the gift-wrapped box? It's very tempting to untie the ribbon and unwrap the speckled wrapping paper, isn't it?

These pretty candle cookies promise to light up your party.

First trace the outlines, then fill in.
Add the speckles using page 24 as your guide.

First create the body of the candle and the flame, then overlay the melting wax.

Place the point for the letter "i" after affixing the whole word to the cookie.

Congratulations

Words are very fragile, so squeeze out in bold strokes.

CHRISTMAS

These cheerful ornaments surely make you
look forward to Christmas, don't they?

Why stop at gingerbread men and snowflakes?
Making an entire cookie house fringed in snow is a sweet endeavor.

The lines of this snowflake are fine and fragile. It may take some practice to get them this thin, but keep trying.

Cut out your cookies using the shapes of the house provided—the walls and roof. When assembling the house, use a medium-consistency icing to glue the edges in place. This will form a tidy shape. When the house is complete, affix the door and windows made of icing. For the snowy roof, squeeze out icing with a consistency that is slightly thinner than medium, then use a fine-tipped paintbrush to render a soft, smooth look.

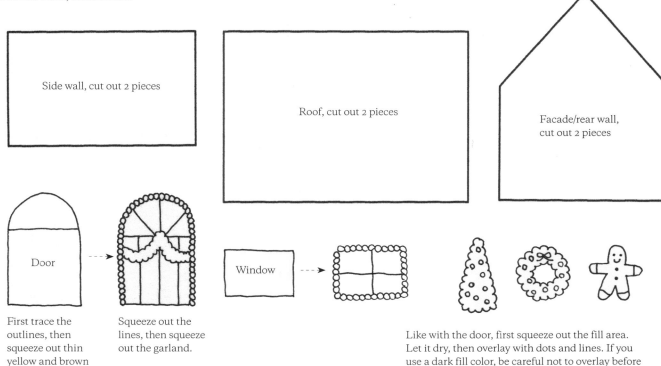

Side wall, cut out 2 pieces

Roof, cut out 2 pieces

Facade/rear wall, cut out 2 pieces

Door

First trace the outlines, then squeeze out thin yellow and brown icing for the fill.

Squeeze out the lines, then squeeze out the garland.

Window

Like with the door, first squeeze out the fill area. Let it dry, then overlay with dots and lines. If you use a dark fill color, be careful not to overlay before the icing dries or else it will become smudgy.

VALENTINE'S DAY

A message of pure love is conveyed through elegant lace
and a heart-shaped cookie.

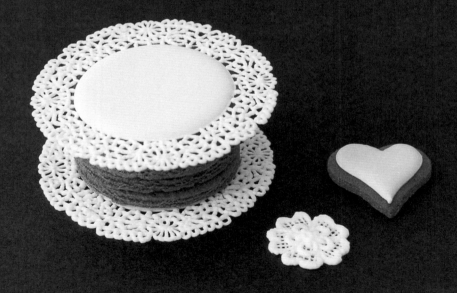

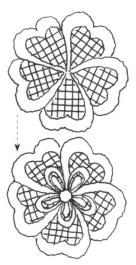

To make the petal rim appear lace-like, squeeze out in a swinging motion by moving the pastry tip from side to side. Then squeeze out the lattice pattern. It's okay if your design doesn't match the picture, since it's very difficult to create an exact match. In fact, space the gaps however you like. Squeeze out the inner petals in a similar fashion.

First squeeze out the outline of the inner circle, then the lace portion. Be sure to place the dainty lines of the lace close to each other. Move the pastry tip in a swaying motion to create a ruffly design. Last, pour thin icing inside the inner circle, and let it dry thoroughly.

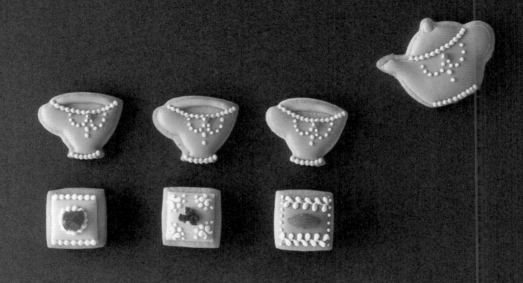

TEA PARTY

Bon appétit! Make your teatime all the more special with these pretty cakes and pink cups of tea.

These cupcake-style cookies are adorned with standing
rose and butterfly decorations for a romantic touch.

Sketches and drawing tips for pages 80 and 81.

Trace the outline, add filler icing,
then complete the pattern by overlaying dots.

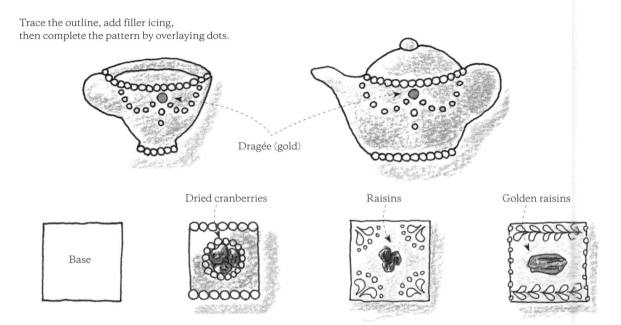

Dragée (gold)

Base

Dried cranberries

Raisins

Golden raisins

The dried fruits should be cut into small pieces before
placing them onto the icing. If a stack of two cookies is
used for the base, you can produce a petit four effect.

To make the cookie cupcake, squeeze out a small amount of thick icing onto the inside bottom of a cupcake wrapper. Securely position a cookie onto the icing. Add a few more cookies one on top of the other, adhering them with small dollop of icing. On the topmost cookie, squeeze out thick icing with a flower-decorating tip, then add the lacy butterfly and rose decorations so that they're upright. Sprinkle on edible gold-leaf sugar before the icing dries.

To create these elegant shapes, follow the directions on page 79. Remember to squeeze out icing by moving the pastry tip in a swaying motion to form a ruffly, striking effect. Since the completed icing is positioned with the side that touches the paper to the front, don't worry about any unevenness on the surface.

A triple-decker wedding cake is just as impressive made with cookies.

The adorable bride and groom make a perfect gift for the newlyweds.

Build the wedding cake by stacking cookies in three different sizes and affixing them to each other with a medium- to thick-consistency icing. Cover the sides by squeezing out thick icing over them, then squeeze out a ring of dots along each of the three rims. Last, embellish with golden dragées and a heart.

First trace the lines, then squeeze out thin icing.

Affix the bird, hearts, and clovers to the window. These designs should be prepared beforehand.